A Video Game Environment of Your Own
Keep out Ma'

Have you ever fantasized about building a video game environment of your own? A place where you and your friends could spend hours and hours playing your favorite games without interruption? Or how about a place that really shows off your game fetish? It's really pretty simple to create such a place and you don't need to rent out a video game hall to do it. This article will introduce a few ideas you can use to build the ultimate gaming center.

The first thing that you want to do is maintain a happy household if you're family member. Trying to play a mean game of Super Mario Tetris or Halo 2 can be impossible with kids running around the house and screaming bloody murder. You won't be able to enjoy the latest role-playing game when the wife's nagging you about bills or undone chores too. Keep a happy home, keep a happy marriage, and your time spent playing video games is heaven away from heaven.

It's no secret that some games require as much concentration and focus as when studying for a calculus exam - and there's nothing more frustrating than when you can't figure out how to get through to "the next level" of a game. This is no time to be distracted and if home life isn't what it could be, you'll never be able to concentrate on your game. Strive to make home a place to unwind first – then work on enjoying your games.

You can next dedicate a place in your home as your exclusive game room. This will not only emphasis the importance that gaming is to you (and to your family members), it will also become conducive to the mentality that you need to play a fun and relaxing (albeit, serious game). Budget permitting, decorate the room with all the amenities that you want. You could add a recliner (or two for your friends), a small stand to hold snacks, a bookcase for your games, and you could even add a small refrigerator and microwave (just in case). Your intent here is to declare the space as yours and that it serves only one purpose: pure gaming pleasure.

What you're after is a place that's completely and totally pleasing to you, both aesthetically and functionally so that you'll enjoy your time there.

With your own space dedicated to gaming, you'll want to do what's necessary to maintain it and keep it in a condition that's inviting not only for yourself, but for others as well. Keep your equipment and games clean. Take care to keep wires from tangling and organize your magazine subscriptions, books, or Internet cheatsheet printouts. Maintenance is a task that doesn't have to burden you as long as you make a daily routine of it. The advantages of keeping a regular maintenance schedule shows that this space is important to you and that you have a right to keep it that way.

But take special care not to alienate yourself from the rest of your family. We all can have a favorite hobby and we can even dedicate a special area of the home to that hobby. However it's extremely important to regard this place as a haven – not a hide out. It's not an area to hide from the kids, it's not a place to shun home responsibilities, and it's not a place to live. If this special space is approached in the latter manner, you'll soon discover it as a place of resentment, uncontrollable habit, or even depression. Be careful, schedule time with the family, and enter your playroom at appropriate times. Cooperation from others will then come naturally.

Becoming a Video Game Expert

You've Got The Skills, So Why Not?

If you find yourself playing video games day-in and day-out, you might be a prime candidate for establishing yourself as a gaming expert. All you need is a good knowledge of a wide range of games and gaming systems, and of course, a lot of patience. The rewards are phenomenal and in the end, you'll be a better person for it.

So what is an expert anyway? Just what is it that qualifies anyone to be an expert on anything? Since there aren't any colleges that offer degrees in this genre, we can qualify any gamer as an expert who has the qualities described above. So if you have the knowledge or ability to play a game skillfully – and you enjoy solving problems, you could probably claim the rights to an expert status.

Just be sure that you ensure your own growth in the gaming industry. Part of being an expert is admitting that there's always more to learn and in the gaming industry, this should never be a hard thing to pull off.

By exposing yourself to new games and new game systems, you can turn every opportunity to play with one into an opportunity to learn more than what you already know. In doing so, you'll learn tons of new strategies and widen your resourcefulness as a point of help to others.

You could also make multiple efforts to collaborate with others involved with video games. Get off the game and get out into the public so that you can network and discuss your discoveries with others. Networking gives you the wonderful opportunities to share or swap secrets, teach others, and learn a little something new at the same time. And the relationships that you build as a result are simply invaluable. There's probably no other way you could gain access to little known gaming secrets than to network among the best gamers around.

If you're completely dedicated toward becoming a gaming expert, consider taking some classes in game programming. Seek out and apprenticeship and find training programs that are offered in both your local area and the gaming industry as a whole. This is an excellent way to learn everything anyone would ever want to know about gaming, and its a good entrance into the gaming industry if you aren't too crazy about making a commitment to a full time gaming career.

You could also subscribe to gaming magazines, participate in online discussion boards, or sign up for book clubs that focus on gaming material.

Take note that your status as a gaming expert may not always be appreciated. Strong criticisms - whether right or wrong – come with the glory of being perceived as the "answer to everything." As an example, you may be rejected for an opportunity that you feel you're perfect for, or you may experience the spew of a less-than-experienced heckler. The first rule of thumb is to not take rejection or spew personally. People may be jealous of your position, or they may want to test you just to see how much you really do (or don't) know. The reasons behind these reactions to your assistance don't really matter as long as you're confident about the quality and value behind your help. A true expert looks past these things and they constantly look for ways to improve themselves.

Buying Video Games for a Gaming Tot

A Quick How To

Visit any video game outlet and you're bound to get overwhelmed by the hundreds of choices available – especially if you're new to gaming. Interestingly, children and teens seem to know their way around these places as if they were their second home. But for the adult, the typical video store looks like some sort of color paint explosion and sooner or later, all the games start to look the same. This guide is for the adult who's buying a game for a younger person perhaps as a birthday gift or as a bribe. Whatever the reason, you're going to appreciate the following tips.

1. Research this strange phenomenon before setting foot inside a video store. There's plenty of information available about video games online, so to reduce frustration offline, fire up your web browser and do a little homework. Visit the website of the gaming outlet nearest you and then look for a link to the games section of the system that your youngster plays. Here's a helpful chart to explain what all those strange letters mean.

    Wii = Nintendo's Wii System
    EA Sports = Entertainment Arts System

PS3 = Playstation 3 System
XBOX 360 = Microsoft's XBOX 360 System
PC = Personal Computer
PS2 = Playstation 2 System
PSP = Playstation Portable System
DS = Nintendo's DS System

The key is to locate the system on the store's website first. The system, it's accessories, and all of the games that work on that system will follow. If not, you may need to use the website's internal search engine.

2. After locating the appropriate games section for your youngster's machine, check out the ratings of each game and create a temporary shopping list of age appropriate material. The Entertainment Software Rating Board (ESRB) gives each game a rating in an effort to inform parents what their children are playing. Here's a handy reference to what the ratings mean:

C = Appropriate for Early childhood
E = Appropriate for Everyone
E 10+ = Appropriate for Everyone aged 10 and older
T = Appropriate for Teens
M = Appropriate for Mature Adults

3. Within your temporary shopping list, try find a game that's built from the latest movie release.

Little people love the new animated movies put out by Disney and Pixar, and they really enjoy re-living precious moments in the movie in a video game. That's why when these movies come out on DVD, their producers put a few games in the "Special Features section" of the CDs.

4. If you can't find a game that's built from a movie that the child likes, try to find a game that centers around a popular cartoon character or one that attempts to educate.

5. If you still can't find one that resembles something that you've heard this particular person rambling on about, first give yourself a slight slap on the hand. You should pay better attention. Then point your browser to the nearest Blockbuster or Hollywood Video website. Follow the same procedure outlined in steps 1 – 3 only this time, elect to rent 5 or 6 games that look appealing. This will give your tot a chance to play some games and select one to keep forever while you return the others.

6. If on the other hand, you did find a game in step 3 or 4, you can either check out online, or drive up to the store and buy it there.

They say you can't judge a book by its cover, but the illustrations on the both video and pc game cases do a pretty good job of representing the game's content. So if you see an illustration of fighting warriors, chances are the game will be more violent than you prefer. If on the other hand, you see an illustration that resembles what you'd see on the cover of an interesting children's book, the game should be age appropriate.

Dealing With Teen Video Game Obsession

Games can be addictive – But obsession is something else.

The following article is meant for parents of a teen who might be obsessed with video and/or computer games. While in some of our other articles we may sound as though we encourage obsession, we share a concern over teens who tend to shun other interests in life in favor for gaming activities to the point where they withdraw from society. We would never encourage this kind of behavior, and that's why we've taken time to describe some of the signs of game obsession and offer some advice on how to deal with it.

Recognizing the signs of teen game obsession isn't as easy as one thinks. It always starts off as first, an interest, and it then starts to grow into an addition. The problem with identifying the beginning stages of game obsession begins with the teen. By the time our children are 15 and up, they've learned some rather impressive debating skills. So when we question their motivations for repetitive game play, they may rebut our concerns with logic and even make it a point to question our own flaws as parents.

Since no parent ever really wants to admit a flaw, we can sometimes cave in and convince ourselves that maybe 4 hours in front of a video game isn't that bad. After all, we spend that much time at the computer, on the phone, or transmitting data back and forth between our Palms, Blackberries, and Cingular cell phones.

Be careful not to fall prey to the logical teen. Video games can be addictive and if the time spent playing them is not carefully monitored, they'll consume everything that a teen used to care about.

The moment you notice your teen's grades falling, homework missing, or social life starting to drop off, nip that game time in the bud. If you wait too late to restrict game time, you may experience pre-adult temper tantrums that you aren't prepared to handle correctly (cursing, breaking things, stealing, running away from home, etc.). At this point, the child is obsessed and will do anything to get his or her hands on a game controller.

Another sign of obsession is a behavioral change. A child obsessed with gaming will lose patience with things and with others, be quick to anger, and react to situations without fully thinking of the consequences. If you've paid any attention to video and/or computer games, you'll notice that they require this kind of behavior to win or to advance to a higher level.

It's unfortunate, but a teen obsessed with this kind of violent gaming is literally being trained to react in the manner described above. That's why it's pertinent that as an adult, you restrict access to this kind of entertainment and replace it with activities that slow thinking (such as art, music, theater, etc.) and expose your child to other non-violent pleasures (swimming, dance, skating, etc.).

There are a lot of debates circulating around about the impact that video games have on today's youth and some of it might warrant paying closer attention to. As a mother or father of a teen, you will do well with your teen's desire to "get his game on" by keeping a close eye out for undesirable changes.

Educational Opportunities in Video Games

There's Lessons in Them Thar Games!

Who would have ever thought that video games - a form of entertainment – could improve the minds of those that play them! The truth is that amid all the cool graphics, the fantastic music, and the intriguing plots, educational opportunities are abound - and to find them, one only needs to look at them a little closer.

1. Video games improve strategic thinking. Rare is the video game that doesn't require its player to make a decision two or three steps ahead of a current situation. With constant play, players quickly learn the advantage of strategic thinking and they start to apply it to actual world opportunities.

2. Video games improve problem solving. Although the same could be said about any game, video games have proven in study after study to improve problem-solving skills. This is because most (if not all) games are centered around a problem and then challenge the player to solve it. In just one game, a player may solve anywhere

16

from three to a hundred or more different problems.

3. Video games improve hand and eye coordination. If you find this hard to believe, pick up a game controller and try to maneuver around the game. Manipulating a game controller demands the same skills that it takes to maneuver a mouse around a computer screen.

4. Video games facilitate quick decision-making. One quality of video games that lends to quick decision making is its impromptu situations. The element of surprise is always around the corner and it's what makes games exciting to play. To win however, players must be able to make smart decisions within a very short amount of time.

5. Video games feed the imagination. We don't really understand the argument against things like television, videos, and gaming where people use the lack of imagination to support their part of the debate. Some people claim that video games take away from the imagination because games supply the mind with things instead of encouraging the mind to come up with these things on their own. Bear in mind that these are the same people who say a stack of blocks is sufficient to grow a child's imagination. Of course we couldn't disagree more. The imagery in video games only fuels the imagination and gives it a spring board to form

new possibilities that might not have occurred otherwise.

6. Video games encourage exploration. In role-playing games, players must venture off the beaten path and explore the unknown. They have to open doors without knowing what's behind them. They have to enter areas of the game without knowing the consequence. And they have to interact with characters that they've never met before. Inside these particular kinds of games, the opportunity to gather up the courage to explorer unknown territory isn't just available, it's required.

7. Video games enforce memorization. Another feature of video games is its strong influence on memorization. The terrain portrayed inside some of these games is huge, yet accessing the maps can be cumbersome and disruptive to the game. To compensate, gamers will not only memorize a large portion of the terrain, they'll remember the tasks required to get to specific areas.

8. Video games teach consequence. All computer and video games operate off of an "action – reaction" principle. Do something, and the game will react. This is a great opportunity to learn about consequence - whether this opportunity is experienced from a gamer's point of view or a

programmer's point of view.

9. Video games teach patience, dedication, and endurance. No great game can be conquered in a day. In fact, some of the best and most popular games take weeks or months to finish.

These are just some of the educational opportunities hidden inside video and computer games. After closer investigation, we're sure you can find more in addition to hours of fun and amazement.

Finding Employment in the Video Game Industry

In another article, we described a great number of educational opportunities that lay hidden in video gaming. This time, we're going to introduce a few employment opportunities as well.

1. Working as a Video Game Clerk. Working at video game store or rental place – either permanently or temporarily – has got to be a teen gamer's dream. In a single place, employees have access to the first games and game systems hot off the market and they're privy to peek inside magazines hot off the press before anyone else. If that wasn't enough, gaming clerks get a discount on what would otherwise be too expensive (games, game systems, and game accessories) to even think about buying. Sweet!

2. Working as a Game Tester. Before a game hits the market, it has to go through extensive testing and if you think the programmers behind the game test their own material, think again. The gaming industry is extremely sensitive about what it puts out into the public. In an effort to remain competitive, it must make absolutely sure that the games it produces work as intended. This is where

testers enter the picture. But it isn't easy to become a game tester. Becoming a game tester requires a little inside help but once you're in there, you'll not only have access to games that no one else knows about, you'll also have an opportunity to shape the game into an experience that you and your comrades prefer.

3. Working as a Game Designer. Do you have good artistic skills? Can you whip out a character faster than you can say, "I drew that"? If so, you may be able to get a career designing video games. Today's video games exude some of the most beautiful graphics ever seen and if you have a good imagination, are able to use some of the most advanced graphics software programs available, and can follow instructions, you could see your own artwork in the next popular video game.

4. Working as a Game Critic. The gaming industry is always looking for good content and if you have a flair for writing combined with a love for games, you could write for game magazines like Game Informer or you could write content for a highly popular gaming website.

5. Working as a Game Programmer. Not a career for everyone, a good game programmer is always in demand. As player preferences change and new technology is developed, someone with the right programming skills has to be there to fill the gap

between what players want, and what the gaming industry can supply. Becoming a game programmer requires extensive training in several different development languages - so if you don't have a clue as to what we just said, skip this profession and look into some of the others.

The great news about all of this is that the gaming industry shows no sign of disappearing any time soon. Even colleges are getting in on the gaming craze as they fill their course books with game programming classes and game design curriculums. There will always be an opportunity for you to blend your love for games with a steady paycheck as long as you remain dedicated to looking for these opportunities, and you make an effort to stay abreast of what's happening in the gaming world.

Check the employment section of your local paper for more, or visit the nearest college to find out what classes and training are available.

Getting New Ideas for Video Games (Part 2)
A Springboard for Video Game Developers

Creating video games is an art, no doubt. The problem is that it isn't easy to come up with ideas for video games. And even when we do get an idea, it doesn't seem as fresh or exciting as we want it to be. The following offers a few ways you can generate some creative ideas to keep your video game as fun to play from beginning to end.

7. Play the video game before it has begun development. That sounds crazy, but it can be done and it's an excellent way to get the plot down. To make this work, relax yourself and visually imagine that you're playing the game from start to finish. Let your mind suggest scenes, characters, plots, and strategies. Write down the game as its being played before your mind, and then repeat for each twist that you'd like to see implemented in the actual game.

8. Throw the plot into the mixer. There could probably be nothing more challenging in a video game than plot twists. As long as it's not too

confusing to the point where players complain and quit playing, rearranging its plot could lend to some fun mind-bending twists that no one would ever predict. Try putting the game's beginning in the middle, or introduce all the subplots in the beginning of the game and have it all start to make sense toward the end (Think, "Pulp Fiction").

9. Look at the game with someone else's eyes. You may already know how you want your game to play, but so may everyone else. To inject some real creativity into your video game, design it as if it were presented from the eyes of a child, a lizard, or an inanimate object like a television. This exercise will not only keep the game intriguing for it's players, it will also keep its development challenging and interesting for you! Don't be surprised if your newfound view changes the game throughout its development. A new perspective has an interesting habit of creating new purposes and new solutions.

10. Challenge the rules. Try to remember that most advances in anything (not just video games) came about from challenging the rules. To make this work, think of the rules imposed on video game developers in the past and just break them! Do the opposite. Where they say you can't or you shouldn't – go on

and do it. As long as your rule-breaking spree causes no harm and doesn't jeopardize the integrity of the game, try it!

11. Don't call your project a video game. Sometimes when you change the name of something, you start to view it differently. This is because different words move a line of thought into a different direction – a different direction that sparks new ideas.

12. Combine ideas. We're often told to ditch the first, second, or even third idea that we come up with for a project in favor for a much stronger idea. But instead of ditching these ideas, why not combined them into one. Combining ideas is one of the easiest ways to come up with new ideas and you can do the with your game. You could combine life forms, scenery, and all kinds of things. The end result would be nothing short of amazing and all the while, your players will wonder, "How did they come up with this stuff?!"

Getting New Ideas for Video Games (Part 3)
A Springboard for Video Game Developers

Creating video games is an art, no doubt. The problem is that it isn't easy to come up with ideas for video games. And even when we do get an idea, it doesn't seem as fresh or exciting as we want it to be. The following offers a few ways you can generate some creative ideas to keep your video game as fun to play from beginning to end.

13. Do the unexpected. This is probably one of the hardest things for linear programmers to do because as software developers, programmers are trained to keep everything working in some sort of straight, logical order. To make this work, game programmers are going to have to give themselves permission to go nuts - to do the unexpected and not obsess over the consequences. As good training for all of us, doing the unexpected is a freeing experience that opens our minds to workable possibilities we probably wouldn't consider otherwise. These are possibilities that could make your video stand out from the crowd of copy-cats.

14. Design the video game for a specific audience. Choose a unique audience to design your game for and make sure that every character, scene, subplot, and strategy caters to the interest of this audience. But don't pick a typical audience – go crazy. Design your game as if a dog were the player, a computer mouse, or even a stack of pancakes. Let your imagination go wild and you'll see a new world unfold before you.

15. Imagine that you're the video game. If you were the video game that you're designing, how would you want to be played? Attempting to answer this question should set you off on quite a creative spree of new and original ideas (if not one hell of a giggling session). Don't just throw the goofy ideas that you get from this exercise into the trash bin. Seriously think of how to implement them into your video game. This strategy is sure to put you on the gaming map.

16. Substitute. Using one object in the place of another is another sure way of coming up with cool ideas for video game, and in certain situations, it's the only way to dream up something fresh and new. When it seems that you just can't come up with a new slant, you're best bet is to replace a typical, predictable character with a lively, cute and helpful soda can. Or replace a typical, predictable plot with some bizarre

scene out of a dream. Remember: nothing is irreplaceable.

17. Introduce a little randomness into the mix. There's a lot to be said about random events. They always bring us the element of surprise and you can use it to keep your video game exciting. The key to making randomness work in a video game is to introduce a set number of possibilities into several sections of the game and then have each of those possibilities lead to a different outcome. Sure, this could drive a player crazy, but you've got to admit, it will send them scrambling for a solution and talking about your game for days.

In the last section of this four-part article, we bring you two more ideas before coming to a close.

Getting New Ideas for Video Games (Part 4)
A Springboard for Video Game Developers

Creating video games is an art, no doubt. The problem is that it isn't easy to come up with ideas for video games. And even when we do get an idea, it doesn't seem as fresh or exciting as we want it to be. The following offers a few ways you can generate some creative ideas to keep your video game as fun to play from beginning to end.

18. Don't finish developing the game. Wouldn't that be a hoot! Instead of developing a video game that has a beginning and an end, design a game that continuously loops with challenges (levels) that increase with difficulty on every round. Winning a game like this would be a matter of racking up points and to satisfy game play, you could have the game post the name of the player with the highest points to a community website. (Hey, it's a thought!)

19. Exaggerate, Exaggerate, Exaggerate. One way to generate ideas for a video game is to exaggerate the characters, scenes, plots, and strategies that you already have down. This is how 'nice" turns into 'cool' and how 'cool' turns into 'awesome.' The trick

is to know when you're crossing the line and going from "possible" to "impossible." You always want to keep a sense of possible reality in a game, however on the same token, you don't want to make the game so possible that it's predictable. There's a delicate balance and as a game developer who wants to stand out from the crowd, you've got to know how far you can stretch this balance without being offensive, silly, or stupid.

The basic point that we want to stress throughout this guide is that your game development doesn't have to follow the status quo. If you stick to what's been done before or what's been played before, you'll find that your games will collect dust on the shelves and that all your time and efforts will have been for naught.

Break established customs or doctrines and you'll get noticed. Get noticed and you'll gain a reputation for developing the most outstanding games around. Being able to get good ideas for your video games ideas is a gift - especially since good ideas can be hard to come by. But stop and think about what you have so far. Is it the best? Could it be better? Would a different approach help you obtain the fame that you crave?

Take a look at each strategy we've introduced in this article and see if you can't implement just one or two of them. Implementing ALL of them would certainly be a challenge, but so would the end result: your game.

Today's gamer craves the unknown, he craves something new, different, and original. If you're suffering from the "blank page syndrome," just pull up our article and consider each strategy as the answer. Expand your current ideas to the point where they excite even you – the developer.

And always remember that your video game is an extension of you. It deals with self-expression, creativity and communication. Don't underestimate yourself or your capabilities to do the unthinkable. And whatever you do – don't underestimate your players. The advantages of following our suggestions far outweigh any doubts you may have because once you step out of the realm of expectations, you make a wonderful contribution to the world.

Getting New Ideas for Video Games (Part 1)
A Springboard for Video Game Developers

Creating video games is an art, no doubt. The problem is that it isn't easy to come up with ideas for video games. And even when we do get an idea, it doesn't seem as fresh or exciting as we want it to be. The following offers a few ways you can generate some creative ideas to keep your video game as fun to play from beginning to end.

1. Make it funny. Humor has a wonderful way of transforming the seemingly dreadful boring into something that's not only tolerable, but engaging as well. And if boredom is an illness, laughter is its cure. If you can inject jokes, funny imagery, or goofy characters into your game, your players will relax and associate your game with good feelings – a definite formula for success.

2. Let your mind wander off the beaten path. Since much of our thinking is associative anyway, there's no reason why you couldn't manifest this association into your video game. When one idea makes you

think of another, include it as part of a video game no matter how illogical the connection is (at first). Remember that video games are your platform for creativity. It's time to be a little wild and a little unconventional. Without this free-form thinking, we surely wouldn't have the creative gems that we have today. You can always restore a sense of logic back into the game at an appropriate time.

3. Make your dreams come true. Literally, turn your dreams into video game scenarios. Had a nightmare lately? Include the scary thing in the game. Had a ridiculously stupid dream lately? Include it in the game as a detour or distraction. Sometimes dreams can be more interesting as life, and as a video game developer, you want your games to be the same. Keep a dream journal and write down those bizarre experiences you have at night. Your gamers will thank you for it.

4. Copy nature. Let's be honest - Nature is pretty weird. We have bees flying around and pollinating plants. We have water evaporating into the sky and then falling down from clouds as rain. Childbirth is a strange phenomenon itself, and germs – the smallest thing on the planet can bring down a herd of elephants. If you could emulate some of this crazy

stuff in your own video games, you will have done what every man secretly wishes he could do himself. And that's take nature into your own hands and shape it into the reality you want! But don't copy nature faithfully. Twist it around. For example, instead of bees flying around and pollinating plants, your video game could have 3-inch aliens flying around and pollinating brainwashed FBI agents. Starting to get the idea?

5. Dig into History. Another good resource for video game material is our own history – but not the boring stuff. We're talking about the good stuff. The embarrassing stuff. Look for odd and weird news online and include the asinine things that people have done in the past as part of your game's plot. Your players won't believe what they're seeing!

6. Go Metaphor Happy. Metaphors are figures of speech in which expressions are used to refer to something that it does not literally denote. It simply suggests a similarity. We're not sure, but we're pretty convinced that a lot of the space ships in video games are based on what we call the "nuts and bolts" metaphor. If you look closely at the designs of some of these vehicles, and then look at some of the tools you have in your toolbox, you'll start to see a

similarity among the two like we did. You can do the same in your video games to come up with some really unique imagery and situations.

Going Broke Playing Games
You Don't Have To And Here's How

If you haven't looked at the cost of new computer or video games and gaming systems as a whole recently, you might be in for a shock. Today's games and gaming systems can run from a meager $30 all the way to a whopping four hundred dollars or more. To a loving mother of a game obsessed teenager, the costs can be astronomical and nothing short of frightening. Fortunately the cost of buying quality computer or video games (including the systems that they run on) can be significantly reduced once you know what to do and where to look.

One alternative to funding a gaming pursuit with a second mortgage is to "go old." By "going old," we mean buying last month's or year's games and game systems. If you could admit the one truth that we all know, but never readily face, you could literally save hundreds of dollars in an instant. This truth is that unless you're a millionaire, none of us can afford to buy the latest toy on the market. The ugly fact behind that truth is that within a relatively short amount of time (say, 60-90 days?), that latest toy will be replaced with a new and improved system, which consequently, grants access to what was wanted in the first place – at half the price! So go old and have a little patience. Within about three to four months, you will have made a tremendous saving.

When it comes to computer gaming, you could also come out better by upgrading games rather then an entire computer. It can take anywhere from a year or more for a gaming company to release a new version and chances are, the upgrade doesn't require new hardware – it just requires a new payment. Remember, the gaming industry can't really keep up with the computer industry either (no one can), so there's no reason to panic or worry. Concentrate on keeping your game current rather than your system. Only in rare instances, such as if your computer is archaic to begin with, will you need to upgrade your hardware. Shop wisely and you can catch a new soundcard, joystick, or graphics card on sale. But if you have a high gigahertz processor and Direct X 9 installed, you'll do fine for quite a while.

Here's a whopper of an idea and one that probably won't take as much of an effort to convince younglings to do as you might think. But to curb the costs of gaming, perhaps a group of families could pitch in and share the finances together Depending on the number in a group, the cost of a new gaming system - and 5 or 6 of the most popular games - could diminish to 20% or more of their original costs.

And since gaming consoles are getting smaller and smaller, there's no reason why a group of families couldn't band together and trade gaming space within their homes every week or two. This way the kids in the neighborhood can enjoy one or two of the new systems on the market that they could never otherwise afford, and they can enjoy them without their parents having to shoulder the burden of funding them alone.

Seeing that kids generally play games together anyway, a group effort of this sort satisfies game cravings at a significantly reduced cost and it keeps everyone happy.

Got Dial Up?

Forget Online Gaming

Computer games have come a long way since electronic checkers and the like. Today, we've got computer games that would put some 21st century movies to shame and interest in online gaming is catching on like some kind of crazy fever. Once dominated by males aged 25 and older, today's gaming generation includes mom, sis, aunt, even grandma and grandpa! If you think you've caught the online gaming bug, and you're thinking about becoming a participant, don't even think you can join in on this online fun using a dial up Internet connection!

Part of the fascination with online gaming lies in its speed. During play, online gaming becomes a virtual world and in order to project a sense of reality into the mix, its games are fast, its movements are smooth, and its sounds are as realistic as we hear them in the natural world. Sitting in front of an online game, and actively participating in one puts the player in another world – a world that's so different, so cool, and so real.

No, we're not talking about a super-fancy version of checkers or backgammon. We're not talking about a visually rich game of tic-tac-toe. We're talking about full-fledged networked or multiplayer gaming that allows anyone to entertain themselves and hoards of others across the world at the same time. Multiplayer games play over online but trust us when we say any old Internet connection won't do.

If you want to get in on this craze, you're going to have to ditch the old dial up connection that you might have and get into broad band. A broadband Internet connection will give you the ability to send and receive highly detailed and realistic imagery at an appropriate speed. It will give you the means to watch videos in real time, and it will allow you to experience speech as if each and every other player were speaking to you directly.

A dial up Internet connection just can't handle this kind of fun, but you can get a broad band connection just as easily. For the techies out there, broadband is a type of data transmission in which a single medium (wire) can carry several channels at once. For the rest of us, broadband is an Internet connection that allows several people to send and receive data at the same time. A dial up connection doesn't do that. A dial up connection can either send or receive – but it certainly can't do both. Let's talk about Broadband ISDN for a minute.

ISDN stands for integrated services digital network and it can transmit transmitting voice, video and data over fiber optic telephone lines at about 64 Kbps (64,000 bits per second).

Most ISDN lines offered by telephone companies give you two lines at once, called B channels. You can use one line for voice and the other for data, or you can use both lines for data to give you data rates of 128 Kbps, three times the data rate provided by today's fastest modems.

Broadband ISDN – a combination of regular broadband and ISDN can transmit voice, video and data over fiber optic telephone lines at about 1.5 million bits per second (bps). It's a much faster connection than either broadband or ISDN alone! If your ISP offers Broadband ISDN, ask for it – your online gaming adventure will be the better for it.

Keeping on Top of Gaming News

The gaming industry is a *huge* industry that consumes as much news space as any other widely known enterprise. It's so large in fact, if you take a walk down the aisle of any store that sells magazines, you'll find at least two or three gaming magazines to select from – and this includes stores that you would least expect to find them in, like the Walgreens Drug Store for Pete's sake.

What's even better, is that regardless of what your skill level with games is, you can take advantage of this news coverage and use what you learn to improve you knowledge, your equipment, and your play. You can additionally find out about gaming events that you can attend or even participate in.

To start, take a trip to your local game shop. Game Crazy and Game Stop are two popular gaming stores that regularly carry related magazines (although you may discover that your local game shop carries only one). One of the things that you'll want to do while looking over these magazines is to compare prices of both games and game systems. The Gamer Informer magazine shows no preference, and provides a one to two inch thick critique of the newest stuff out there. Inside this resource, you'll find commentary on the Wii, EA games, the PS3, the Xbox 360, PC games, the PS2, the PSP and the DS system.

As a no holes barred manual to what's hot and what's not, gaming magazines show you how news in the mainstream media affects game production and how it can affect not only your purchase decisions, but the type of games you play as well. It isn't uncommon for a game to experience a rise in sales just from being mentioned in the 5:00 news hour.

You could learn what's happening with new and competitive gaming businesses before investing in their products, however if you dig a little deeper, you can even find out what's influencing the market that you're a part of.

Here's an example of what we mean:

"Today, professional gaming took a giant leap forward. DIRECTV, Inc., the nation's leading digital service provider and key partners are taking the professional

gaming industry to the next level with the creation of a new video gaming professional sports league that will be the standard for the industry and redefine the consumer gaming experience."

You can also discover what influence the news has on gaming within an international level:

"The British Academy of Film and Television Arts today announced that its 2007 British Academy Video Games Awards will be held on the evening of Tuesday 23 October at Battersea Evolution in London."

Interested in console specific information? How about Nintendo:

"Nintendo plans to boost Wii production (AP via Yahoo! News) Nintendo's president acknowledged Friday that the shortage of the hit Wii game machine was "abnormal," and promised production was being boosted to increase deliveries by next month."

Of course, there's always the chance that you'll find out things you're weren't exactly supposed to find in the first place:

"Halo 3 gameplay leaked online (The Inquirer) A VIDEO HAS has appeared online showing seven minutes of fresh, crisp Halo 3 gameplay."

From these few, small examples, you've learned about the creation of a new video gaming professional sports league, the Academy Video Games Awards, a boost in Wii production, and the leak of a "certain" video from a "certain" game. Just imagine what you'd find out with a monthly subscription to GamePro (www.gamepro.com), Computer Games Magazine (www.cgonline.com), or GameSlice (www.gameslice.com)!

Online Gaming
For Mom and Dad...

Have you ever wondered what your child was rambling on about at the dinner table when he or she started saying things like "VR" or "RPG"? If so, you're not alone. "VR" and "RPG" aren't new text messaging acronyms – they're acronyms for gaming and this article is going to introduce you to some of the more common forms.

If you at least thought of the Internet when you heard "VR" or "RPG" however, you're on the right track. Exclusive to the online environment, "VR" or "RPG" – which consequently stands for virtual reality gaming and role playing games – are just two aspects of a gaming world gone wild. The days of playing scrabble in front of the fireplace are over in today's generation, but we don't believe you'll hear too many people complaining about it. Today's generation is fascinated with online gaming – an opportunity to play games over the Internet with hundreds of people at a time.

Available to anyone with a computer and fast Internet connection, there are thousands of online games available to play by anyone... sometimes free and sometimes for a fee. They range from the familiar family board games to strange and more complicated games which require a hundred page manual to understand. One thing that they all have in common however is that they're fun to play.

The most common type of online game you'll probably run into is the Flash game - usually located on educational sites or Yahoo! for Kids for example. These games may or may not involve other players, but they're always full of color, they're fast to download, and they're fun to play. Since they run inside the web browser, no special equipment is needed. These are the simple games – more intriguing than checkers, but no more difficult to play than chess.

Another type of online gaming is more violent than the ones we described above and it's similar to the "shoot-em-up" type games found on the first Nintendo and Playstation systems. Designed from the first person's point of view, the player typically maneuvers around the screen as a weapon-clad hand – periodically changing weapons as the game's scenario permits. The violence in these games vary from mild to offensive, and as a parent, you're cautioned to monitor your children's access to them – especially since these games are played online with other people.

Next, in terms of complication or violence, comes the virtual reality gaming and role playing games that we introduced earlier. These types of games require an extensive amount of time spent online since players assume the role of a game character in play. Players work hard to build up an inventory of weapons or skills – none of which can be accomplished in a period of thirty minutes or less. They then go on to interact with other characters which extends game time even longer (if it even stops). Both virtual reality gaming and role playing games require and encourage strategic thinking, but as parents, you may not be comfortable with the violence that's prominent in some of these games. Nor may you be comfortable with the amount of time that playing these kinds of games can consume. Depending on the complexity of the game, any one person could spend at least six months at a game and having access to thousands of other players simultaneously doesn't exactly make them easy to walk away from.

Our best advice is to learn about these games right along with your child and make the decision to play them (or not play them) together. You can find some helpful advice about making computer decisions with children in our article entitled, "Protecting Children Online."

Playing Online Games Pro-Style
Even if you don't know what you're doing...

One of the most intimidating parts of getting started with online gaming is getting over the fear of screwing things up for other players. It's one thing to play a game and make mistakes at home, but it's an entirely different thing to play a game and make mistakes that can cause failure in the game plays of others. But there's no reason to let this fear stop you or another gaming newbie from having fun. This article will give you the in's and out's of online gaming so that you can start with the confidence you need to continue on.

The first step anyone new to online gaming should take is to first, learn how to play offline. You can read the game's manual and save yourself from seeing the infamous acronym, "RTFM" scroll across your screen. Know what that acronym stands for? It stands for "Read The Fu**ing Manual" and its spewed by serious gamers to vulnerable newbies who interrupt a game with questions like, "What is this place?" or "What am I supposed to do?"

You could search the web for game related discussion groups, FAQ's, and walkthroughs. And you could learn more from game specific Usenet newsgroups. In other words, you could do your "homework." Some of the kind of information you want to learn includes how to play, how to create characters, how to gather equipment, and how to implement some smart strategies. Trust us when we say your gaming comrades will appreciate it!

In addition to reading how to play an online game, you can familiarize yourself with the game's interface. Just as you searched the net for a game's textual instruction, you can additionally search the net for a game's screenshot (or series of screenshots). Having a graphical representation (.gif or .jpg image) of a game on your screen gives you a chance to memorize where all the game's controls are. Knowing where everything is on a game before you play will speed things up not only for yourself, but also for everyone else. No one wants to wait for you to search for an inventory panel or message screen in a game when the location of these items is obvious to everyone else.

Once you start with a game, don't let the pressure of staying in the game prevent you from doing the unthinkable: dying. A character dying in a game is inevitable at certain points, and unless you willingly let go of a lose-lose situation, you'll run the risk of holding the game up for everyone else. It's like a game of chess. If it's checkmate – it's checkmate. Call it a day and start anew. Whatever you do, don't hang around waiting for some magical fairy to come to your rescue. Please let your character die with dignity.

On the same token, you don't want to take dying personally. Remember that online gaming is still just a game. A character that dies in a game is not representative of your character as a person. Turn a death into learning experience. At the very least, you'll learn your way around an online game by learning all the things that you aren't supposed to do!

Above all else, ensure that your computer has what it takes to maintain the current pace of an online game. Don't try to play an online game with a slow computer or slow Internet connection. In fact, if you're still using dial up, find another hobby. A slow processor and connection will ensure instant death because other players aren't going to politely wait for their own defeat. They're going to squash you like a bug.

Hunt around for a computer that was built for online gaming and get a DSL or ISDN Internet connection. You'll need a fast processor, a high quality graphics card, and a sound machine to match.

By following these simple suggestions, you will have passed the "newbie" test and earned respect as a serious gamer much more quickly than if you stumbled your way through what others pride as "the ultimate hobby."

Playing Nice
A Few Suggestions for Gaming Etiquette

No, it isn't Ms. Manners to the rescue, nor is it Polite Polly knocking at your noggin. We just know how easy it is to get frustrated or even angry while playing a difficult game, but if we're not careful, that anger and frustration could lead to some butt-ugly moments during a time that's supposed to be amusing. The following is offered in an effort to keep everything fun and entertaining during a session of group play.

1. Encourage each other. Even if you're competing with each other in a boxing match or car race, take time out to congratulate another player for making a smooth or cunning move. There's no need to be a kiss-up, but when tensions are high, and the desire to impress is high, you can help relax any stress just by throwing out a few compliments here and there.

2. Be patient. Your gaming comrades may not be as fast, as coordinated, or as smart as you. So when you notice your regular game pace slowing down, don't criticize. You could quietly plan your next move or you could offer to help if you notice that

your buddies seem lost. This will encourage cooperation and relive some of the stress involved with playing a difficult game.

3. Take some breaks. Permitting that your group finds appropriate places in a game to pause, take advantage and get up to stretch, snack, use the john, talk about school, or catch a few silly commercials on television. A long stretch of game play is tiring and stressful at the same time.

4. Play an inclusive game. By that we mean to make efforts to ensure everyone in the group contributes to the game's completion. You never want to make another person feel left out or just hanging around to fill the space. Create opportunities for everyone involved to participate and help play.

5. Listen to others. You may think that you know all the answers about a game or game system, but listen to what others in the group have to say. You just might learn something new.

6. Invite the "weird guy." This bit of advice of course comes after the horrid Virginia Tech massacre. Tales circulating this news event indicate that the young man responsible was a loner and the victim of bullying during his teenage years as well. Sometimes, all it takes to prevent things like this is a simple effort to reach out to someone. We're not suggesting that an invitation to a gaming party

would have saved the lives of 33+ college students, but we are suggesting that making an effort to make others feel welcome and wanted is a huge step towards eliminating the isolation known to cause these kinds of senseless acts.

7. Vow to keep the voice level and cursing to a minimum. That almost goes without saying, but to prevent arguments, agree beforehand to not cross the line when it comes to debating about a particular strategy or selecting a game to play. Some of the most serious fights stem from the silliest arguments. But you can prevent a flare up within your group just by maintaining a cool composure during the entire session.

Now see? That's not too bad a list. All the things that we suggested are certainly "do-able" and they really do work to create a calm and enjoyable environment.

Playing Old Games on a New Computer
It's a Hoot!

Admit it – you still crave a good game of scrolling Super Mario or Dig Dug just like you did "back in the day." We all do because playing them brings back some of the fondest memories. But it isn't easy to play these games the way we used to. Unless we've kept the systems and cartridges of the past in good working condition, our only trip down this jagged pixel lane is through a little known gem called emulation.

Through emulation, you can play some of your favorite games from the past including games made for Commodore, Atari, and Nintendo. Emulation refers to the ability of a program or device to imitate another program or device and it tricks the software into believing that a device is really some other device. It is also possible for a computer to emulate another type of computer. For example, there are programs that enable an Apple Macintosh to emulate a PC.

All that gobbledy gook doesn't really mean too much until you discover that with the right emulator, your computer can play all your old favorite games. And the news gets even better. You can download emulators from the Internet – free. You can download Amiga, Commodore, GameBoy, Playstation 1, and Nintendo emulators plus you can download the games (ROMs) that these machines play.

Our favorite emulator is the ZSNES Emulator. This particular program emulates the old Super Nintendo console and you can learn more about it yourself by visiting http://www.zsnes.com. This program comes with an extensive help file and walks you through the process of setting up a copy on your own PC. At the very least, your system needs a 486/100 processor, 14.5MB of RAM, a VGA card, and a Sound Blaster or 100% compatible sound card. However a system with a fast P200 or higher Pentium processor, 32MB of RAM, VGA card, and Sound Blaster 16 or 100% compatible sound card yields the most realistic results.

But don't think that just because a console is on the computer – you can't enjoy your favorite gaming accessories. The ZSNES Emulator let's users maneuver around games with the keyboard and a joystick. But enough about the emulator - You probably want to know what kind of games you can play, right?

Called ROMs, you can play any game on your PC that you played on the Super Nintendo System including:

- Bomberman 5
- Super Battleship
- Beavis n' Butthead
- Bustamove
- Clue
- Dragonballz
- DreamTV
- Final Fantasy 4
- Frogger
- The Great Waldo Search
- Inspector Gadget
- Jeopardy Deluxee
- John Madden Football
- Mariokart
- Marvel Superheroes
- Megamans Soccer
- Mighty Morphin Power Rangers
- Monopoly
- Mortal Kombat 2
- Pinocchio
- Power Rangers

- Race Driving
- Carmen San Diego
- SimAnt
- SimCity
- SimCity 2000
- Super Mario RPG
- Sonic
- Space Football
- Starfox
- Streetfighter 2
- Super Black Bass
- Super Ninja Boy
- Super Punch-Out!!
- Teenage Mutant Ninja Turtles
- Themepark
- Troddlers
- Utopia
- Vortex
- Wacky Race
- Wheel of Fortune
- Wings 2
- Wordtris
- World Soccer 94
- Yoshis Island
- Zelda 3
- ... and tons more.

Downloading these games is a simple matter of finding them online and there are plenty of websites that host them. Try http://www.everyvideogame.com for starters.

Be aware that there's an issue with downloading these games and it's a legal one. Basically, you're not allowed to download and play any game that you don't already own on a cartridge. If can abide by this law, you can revisit the past, in the present, on your brand new PC.

This Game Sucks
A Guide To Giving New Games a Chance

It's hard to get into a new groove once we've settled into a favorite pattern of doing something and that includes playing new games or trying a new game system. It's important to remember however that just because you're not used to the way a new game plays or the way that a new system runs – it doesn't mean that there's something wrong with it. The following offers some advice on how to get over the hurdle of giving new games a chance.

1. Accept the errors of your ways. Nothing is perfect and that includes video games, the system that it plays on, and dare we say – even you! While trying a new game, you're bound to trip all over the place and make even some of the most goofiest mistakes that anyone could ever make. Try to remember that flaws are inevitable and the even the master of all masters (that's you) can blunder your way through a new game. Mistakes don't make you a terrible player. On the other hand, they don't make the game stupid or dumb. In fact, it's quite the opposite. If you find yourself making mistakes during a new game, it's

time that to slow down and give this game a second and more serious look. If something in the game tripped you up – you, the master of all masters – then the game couldn't be as bad as you first thought.

2. Play a new game when you're "in the mood". What a fast-paced world we live in! So fast, that we mistakenly expect to understand a game within the first 5 minutes of putting into the console! Then when we're not sure of what to do, the game becomes confusing, or just dumb. Never try a new game when you're not in the mood to or when you're in a rush. New games require patience and a thorough read of its manual.

3. See the positive. There's something good about every video game – even the more violent ones (although we're not prepared to defend violent video games). While checking out a new game, think about what you like about the game as opposed to what you can't quite figure out what to do yet. A positive attitude will carry on to other aspects of the game and before you know it, you'll be encouraged to carry on with it and make some real progress.

4. Don't be such a know it all. In other words, don't be blinded by your own conceit or skills in a particular genre of games that you close yourself off to new ways of accomplishing tasks. The biggest room is the room for improvement and your room is no exception. Understand that the game you're playing may have something new to teach you about gaming as a whole. Then revel in it.

5. Continue to play. It's highly doubtful that anyone will like a new game in one day. Keep playing a new game until you're absolutely sure that you don't ever want to see it in your console again.

6. Play by yourself. It's quite possible that if you play a new game with a friend, you'll be vulnerable to accepting your friend's feelings about the game as your own. Play a new game by yourself so that you can interpret your own feelings about the game and not anyone else's.

Video Games in the Future
A Gamer's Plea

With video game technology advancing so fast and so far from where it started, one can't help but to entertain the idea of where it's going to go from here. After all, that is part of a larger creative process and we'd like to think that our writings contribute even in some small way. One of the earliest video games that we can remember is Commodore's "Pong." But never did we think the industry would have reached the point where it is today. One thing is for sure however, and that's the gaming is pushing full force ahead.

Today we did a little fantasizing to see where our imagination and desires would take us.

The following offers some suggestions of what could be done short of a little thing called, "impossible."

We're a little intrigued with the "Sun Game Glasses" idea. Wearing a pair of dark sunglasses and using the technology implemented by Nintendo's "Wii" system, we could literally watch a game take place right before our eyes and then interact with it using a device that's about the size of a pen. Since this isn't exactly a new idea, we're curious to watch what develops from University of South Australia's 'ARQuake' project - a springboard for this kind of gaming to develop in the near future for sure.

Another cool idea we'd like to see erupt within the gaming industry is the ability to talk to the characters inside a game. Some games allow players to textually speak to game characters already, but we'd like to see this pushed a little further. We'd like to be able to orally interact with characters: ask questions, joke around, warn and speak to them as if we were speaking to another human being. And we'd like to hear these characters talk back! It's the ultimate artificial intelligence opportunity and although it would probably be years before this technology would be available on a wide scale, we're sure it would be a hit.

Will we ever get to the point where we can play inside a simulated environment the way the characters in Star Trek: The Next Generation could play? Virtual reality is getting close, but the reality of the simulation is gone the moment we put on the silly-looking goggles and gloves. In order for simulation of this sort to work, there has to be as little a barrier between gamers and the game as possible. We don't what to just think we're inside a game, we want to feel that we're inside a game and to be honest, we don't want to have to go somewhere outside our home to do so.

The television or computer screen will suffice for now, but in the future, we're going to want to be surrounded with the elements that make gaming the wonder that it is today. We're going to want to transform our dens or bedrooms into a virtual alien ship or simulated jungle. In short, we want a new world.

One possible obstacle to bringing this fantasy into our living rooms is public acceptance. Would the public be ready for such a high level of entertainment? And could the public handle it? Immediately following Nintendo's Wii release, customers were ready to complain that they wanted their old controller back! So as with any new development, there will surely be unintended consequences and although we're gung-ho for these types of advances, we also share concerns about the impact it would have on an audience that isn't "virtually ready."

As a result, we can certainly envision a few laws introduced that restricted the use of our fantasy gaming. We already have some laws that attempt the same now and in our opinion, that's a good thing. The last thing we want to encounter in gaming is physical harm – especially when we're trying to enjoy virtual entertainment!

What Makes A Great Game
A Gentle Reminder for Programmers

It's easy to get lost in all the details of building a great video or computer game – so easy in fact, that we can forget the parts of a game that make them fun to play. The following serves as a gentle reminder of what prompts players to play games in the first place. Refer to this reminder in the event that you get bogged down or distracted with confusing C++ syntax, or lines and lines of Visual Basic statements and DLL structures.

1. Remember the player is the main character. Here's a secret between you and me: People play games to gain a sense of control. If you can manage to program your game in a way that puts the player in control, then you've already won half the battle. This doesn't mean to suggest that the game should be easy. It simply means that when a gamer runs home from school or drives home from work to play a video game, she wants to feel the control that she didn't have during the hours between nine and five. The outcome of a game – whether it's a win or a loss - should never be random, but the result of a good, controlled game play instead.

2. KISS. Remember that acronym? It stands for Keep It Simple Stupid. We all know that programming a game is hard business, but believe us when we say we don't want to be reminded of it. The difficulty of programming a game should never be part of the game play so when possible, make the game easy to start, easy to navigate, and of course, easy to play. We're not asking for pre-school strategy here, but on the other hand, we don't want to feel as dumb as a pre-schooler either. Forget the hundred page manual. Nobody except the truly obsessed is going to read it anyway. Build your game for the average Joe and everyone will be your fan.

3. Add plenty of action. And add lots of it too. The more action you add to your game, the more attention players will pay attention to it. And the more that players pay attention to your game, the more addictive your game gets. For every action that a player's character makes, have the game react and then prompt the player for more.

4. Make the story a good one. Nothing is worse than playing a game only to wonder what you're doing and why. Purpose is and always has been a human obsession. But without it, we're left wandering... in the darkness... wondering bizarre things like how the

house would look in a coat of bright pink paint. Don't give your players the opportunity to waste time like that. Give them a mission and make sure your game reminds them what the mission is at opportune times and why they must complete it.

5. Give us eye candy. But make it relevant. The graphics in a game shouldn't be distracting, they should make our eyeballs glaze over with satisfaction upon seeing them, and then salivate for more. Graphics should contain clues and entice us further and further into the game until we've beaten the thing.

6. Make it real. Fantasy games are okay, but what makes them cool is the fact that they're realistic. It's hard to get into something that isn't familiar or that there's no way we could ever experience. But if you can implement some reality into your games, players will appreciate it and relate to it on a whole new respectable level.

What's Up With NintendoDS?

A Guide of What's Available for the NintendoDS System

If you're looking for a game system that comes with a butt-load of inexpensive games, you come to the right place. No other gaming system on the market today hosts as many games at such low prices as the handheld NintendoDS System. Nor does any other gaming system on the market cater to such a young audience.

More appropriate for young gamers than teens or adults, NintendoDS games bring back the SuperMario flavor that we've all come to love. Pokemon is still as strong as ever with this system as well, however we've noticed a few new games (and types of games) thrown into the mix too.

This article describes some of the accessories and games available for this particular sytem that everyone can enjoy.

The NintendoDS System. This isn't your regular GameBoy system of yesteryear. The new NintendoDS System has a high-powered flat, folding handheld gaming device complete with bright color touch screen technology – all available for only $129.99.

NintendoDS Accessories. Like the games that this system plays, its accessories are just as plentiful – fully appreciated by the serious gamer on the go. You can get a $14.99 headset for those quiet moments, and sport your system in a small $9.99 Duo game case, $9.99 ultimate leather case, or $17.99 G-Pak for quick trips or for storage. For $29.99, you can stock up on a multitude of accessories encased in a convenient player pack or settle for quick emergency fixes with the $14.99 value kit. Recharging is a breeze on a $9.99 glow deck.

NintendoDS Games. Looking for games? We've separated this part of our guide into two sections: one for children and one for adults. Use caution when purchasing NintendoDS games for players under 18 years of age.

FOR CHILDREN:

Pokemon: Perls $34.99

Pokemon: Diamond $34.99

Pokemon: leaf Green $19.99

Pokemon: Fire Red: $19.99

Pokemon: Emerald: $34.99

Pokemon Ranger $34.99

Pokemon: Mystery Dungeon Blue $34.99

Pokemon: Mystery Dungeon Red $34.99

Yoshie's Island DS $34.99

Wario: master of Disguise $34.99

Big Brain Academy $19.99

Brain Age: Train Your Brain in Minutes a Day $19.99

Nintendogs: Dalmatian & Friends $34.99

Custom Robo Arena $34.99

Diddy Kong Racing DS $ 34.99

Kirby Squeak Squad $4.99

Mario Hoops 3 on 3 $34.99

Mario Kart DS $34.99

Mario Vs. Donkey Kong 2: March of the Minis $34.99

New Super Mario Bros. $34.99

Cats $29.99

Horsez $29.99

Dogz $29.99

Settlers II $29.99

Lost in Blue 2 $29.99

Spectrobes $ 29.99

SNK vs. Capcon Card Fighters $29.99

Purr Pals $29.99

Cooking Mama $19.99

COMING SOON:

Diner Dash

Pony Friends

Dragon Ball Z: Harukanaru

Super Collapse 3

NOTE: Harukanaru's fighting style in the new
version of Dragon Ball Z for NintendoDS differs from

the style in its 2005 predecessor. In Dragon Ball Z: Harukanaru, players battle using the turn-base action formula.

FOR ADULTS:

COMING SOON:

Touch the Dead

NOTE: Touch of the Dead is rated M for Mature Audiences, and exhibits the arcade shooter style. Please remember to follow the guidelines set by the Entertainment Software Rating Board (ESRB) when buying games for children under the age of 18. Here's a handy reference to what the ratings mean:

C = Appropriate for Early childhood
E = Appropriate for Everyone
E 10+ = Appropriate for Everyone aged 10 and older
T = Appropriate for Teens
M = Appropriate for Mature Adults

What's Up With Xbox 360?

A Guide of What's Available for Microsoft's XBox 360 System

The XBox 360 System. The new Xbox 360 console ($399.99) brings Microsoft technology to the gaming industry like never before. This new toy sports new Internet connections to social communities and puts the gamer in ultimate control with goo-gobs of fun accessories.

This article describes some of those accessories and the games available that (almost) everyone can enjoy.

XBox 360 Accessories. For such a powerful system, it should be no surprise that this system takes full advantage of accessorizing. We can start by saving games on the $19.99 512MB memory unit or with the $29.99 64MB memory unit. To keep the power going, we can look at the $29.99 Quick Charge Kit or the smaller $19.99 Play & Charge Kit. On the go, you can carry and use the $11.99 Rechargeable Batter Pack while re-powering you controller with the $29.99 charge Station.

Increase connectivity with the $99.99 Wireless Network Adapter and keep your system "kewl" with the $19.99 Intercooler. But that's enough about maintenance. Let's look at the fun.

Get a $39.99 Wired controller or $49.99 Wireless Controller to play your games. Unless you want feel like getting behind the wheel. In that case, you can try on the $149.99 Wireless Racing Wheel for size.

Want a little multimedia action? Get a $199.99 HD-DVD player (don't forget the $19.99 remote) – a $39.99 Live Vision Camera or a $59.99 Wireless Headset (wired headset available for $19.99). Then jam your way onto the $89.99 Guitar Hero II.

Of course if you want to get down with your PC, check out Xbox's $19.99 Wireless Gaming Receiver and user your Xbox 360 controller on the computer!

XBox 360 Games. Looking for games? We've separated this part of our guide into two sections: one for children and one for adults. Use caution when purchasing XBox 360 games for players under 18 years of age.

FOR CHILDREN:

Xbox's UEFA Champions League 2006-2007 $59.99

Xbox's Viva Pinata $29.99

Xbox's Fuzion Frenzy 2 $29.99

Meet the Robinsons $49.99 (by Disney Interactive Studios)

Xbox's Star Trek Legacy $39.99

Konami's Dance Dance Revolution Universe $49.99

COMING SOON:

Forza MotorSport 2

FOR ADULTS:

Xbox's Halo 2 $29.99 (rated 10 by GameInformer)

Xbox's Gears of War $59.99 (rated 9.5 by GameInformer)

Xbox's Crackdown $59.99 (rated 8.5 by GameInformer)

Capcom's Lost Planet: Extreme Condition $59.99

Bethesda Softworks' Elder Scrolls IV: Oblivion $59.99

Xbox's Rainbow Six: Vegas $59.99 (rated 9.5 by GameInformer)

D3 Publishers' Earth Defense Force 2017 $39.99

Activision's Cabela's African Safari $29.99

Activision's Marvel: Ultimate Alliance $59.99 (rated 9.25 by GameInformer)

Activision's History Channel: Civil War $39.99

Ubisoft's Ghost Recon: Advanced Warfighter 2 $59.99 (rated 8.75 by GameInformer)

Sega's Armored Core 4 $59.99

NOTE: A lot of Xbox 360 games exhibit the RP warning. Please remember to follow the guidelines set by the Entertainment Software Rating Board (ESRB) when buying games for children under the age of 18. Here's a handy reference to what the ratings mean:

C = Appropriate for Early childhood
E = Appropriate for Everyone

E 10+ = Appropriate for Everyone aged 10 and older

T = Appropriate for Teens

M = Appropriate for Mature Adults

RP = Rating Pending (NOT appropriate for children)

The following games sport ESRB's RP rating:

Mass Effect

Shadowrun

Blue Dragon

Tenchu Z

The Drakness

Bioshock

Fantastic Four: Rise of the Silver Surfer

Hour of Victory

What's Up With Playstation 2 and 3?

A Guide of What's Available for SCEA's Playstation 2, Playstation 3, and the PSP System

The Playstation Systems. As number three in a line of Playstation products, Playstation 3 ($599.99) boasts new parallel processing that enables broadband multiplayer action. It's built in Blu-Ray disc drive promises high definition gaming, tons of media storage, streaming videos, music and an online service leaving you little to desire.

It's predecessor, system number two, sells for only $19.99 and networks as well (just not as fast as system number three). With over 1,400 games to choose from, it's hard to argue against this bargain.

PSP is hot again ($169.99) and integrates 3D gaming on widescreen with high fidelity stereo music, full motion video, communication and wireless networking.

Playstation 2 Accessories. If you're still "old schooling" your Playstation, then you'll enjoy Playstation's Dual Shock 2 Analog Controller ($24.99), Wireless NERF controller ($29.99), or it's 8MB memory card ($24.99). But the music doesn't stop there. It plays on with the SingStar Pop game and accessory pack ($49.99) or the Guitar Hero II ($79.99).

Playstation 3 Accessories. What's required? The Playstation 3 system sports two different kinds of controllers: a standard Chillstream controller ($39.99) and a Sixaxis Wireless controller ($49.99). Combined with the Blu-ray remote control ($24.99), you can have complete domination over your system in no time.

PSP Accessories. Never interrupt your game play again with a 2GB Memory Stick Pro Duo ($69.99) or 4Gb Memory Stick Pro Duo ($109.99). Carry your handheld in a Platinum Pack ($19.99) or Traveler Case ($19.99). And don't forget a carry all for your media ($14.99). PSP's Media Manager ($24.99) will keep you organized as well.

Playstation Games. Looking for games? We've separated this part of our guide into two sections: one for children and one for adults. Use caution when purchasing Playstation games for players under 18 years of age.

Playstation 2 Games

FOR CHILDREN:

MLB 07: The Show $59.99

ATV 4: Off Road Fury $39.99

Meet the Robinsons $29.99

Dance Dance Revolution: supernova $39.99

Durnout: Dominator $39.99

NBS Street Homecourt $59.99

FOR ADULTS:

Shadow of the Colossus $19.99

God of War $19.99

Gran Turismo 4 $19.99

Socum U.S. Navy Seals Combines Assault $39.99

Rogue Galaxy $39.99

God of War II $49.99

Destroy All Humans! 2 $39.99

Grand Theft Auto: Vice City Stories $19.99

Grand Theft Auto: San Andreas $19.99

Medal of Honor: Vanguard $39.99

Dawn of Mana $39.99

Elder Scrolls IV Oblivion $59.99

Resistance: Fall of Man $59.99

MotorStorm $59.99

Playstation 3 Games
FOR CHILDREN:

MLB 07: The Show $59.99

NBS Street Homecourt $59.99

FOR ADULTS:

Elder Scrolls IV Oblivion $59.99

Resistance: Fall of Man $59.99

MotorStorm $59.99

NOTE: Elder Scrolls IV Oblivion is works with all Playstations and is a game

COMING SOON:

Lair

Ghost Recon Advanced Warfighter 2

PSP Games
FOR CHILDREN:

Ultimate Board Game Collection $39.99

Street Horizon $39.99

MLB 07: The Show $39.99

Rachet & Clank: Size Matters $39.99

Midnight Club 3: DUB Edition 19.99

Full Auto 2: Battlelines: $39.99

NOTE: Street Horizon brings both turn-based and real-time strategy game play.

FOR ADULTS:

300: March to Glory: $29.99

Socum U.S. Navy Seals Combines Assault $39.99

After Burner Black Falcon $39.99

Dragonball Z Shin Budokai Another Road $39.99

The Warriors $19.99

Grand Theft Auto: Vice City Stories $29.99

Prince of Persia: Rival Swords $39.99

Rocky Balboa $39.99

COMING SOON:

Dungeons & Dragons: Tactics

Ghost Recon: Advanced Warfighter 2

What's Up With Wii?

A Guide of What's Available for Nintendo's Wii System

If you haven't heard of Nintendo's Wii system, we have just one question for you. Where have you been?! This hot new gaming system made its debut right at the time when Microsoft's new Xbox hit the market. But what makes this system so popular is that it's the first system that incorporates virtual reality in the living room. That, in addition to Nintendo's dedication to producing gaming material for that entire family as opposed to the complex games that we have on the market (for other systems) today.

This article describes some of the accessories and games available that everyone can enjoy.

The Wii System. Welcome back to family fun with this console. For only $249, the entire family can enjoy time's treasured games and physically interact with them using Nintendo's unique wrist-strapped controller. Anyone at any skill level can get in on the

fun with this new machine and it comes with a free
Wii Sports game cartridge.

Wii Accessories. If you're still "old school" and you
prefer to use the classic Nintendo style controller, no
need to fret. They're still available and they cost no
more than $19.99. But if you can't wait to try out the
Wii Remote, get one or two or three at only $40 each.
The Wii Nunchuck Controller will run you about
$19.99, however both the Nunchuck and Remote
controller will give you hours of fun as you swing
your way through your favorite games.

Of course, all that gaming could warrant the purchase
of the Wii Air cooler ($14.99) or the Wii Charge
Station ($29.99). And you certainly don't want to quit
a game without saving your place! You can buy a 1GB
SD Memory card ($39.99) or 2 GB SD memory card
($59.99) made by SanDisk, and pick up the fun where
you left off at a later time.

To make sure your Wii console fits snuggly into the
back of your television, you can buy a pack of Wii
Component cables for $29.99.

Wii Games. Looking for games? We've separated this part of our guide into two sections: one for children and one for adults. Use caution when purchasing Wii games for players under 18 years of age.

FOR CHILDREN:

Excite Truck...$49.99

Wario Ware: Smooth Moves........................$49.99

Super Paper Mario.....................................$19.99

Bionicle...$49.99

Sonic and the Secret Rings........................$49.99

Cooking Mama: Cook Off............................$49.99

Tiger Woods PGA Tour 07........................... $49.99

NOTE: Bionicle may not look children friendly at first, but it really is a fun and innocent game that battles and controls a line of toy action figures. It's based on Lego's Bionicle universe. Cooking Mama is rather new to the Nintendo game suite and it challenges young players to prepare more than 300 real recipes from 10 different countries.

FOR ADULTS:

The Legend of Zelda: Twilight Princess......$49.99

Medal of Honor Vangaurd..........................$49.99

The Godfather: Blackhand Edition.............$49.99

COMING SOON:

Mario Party 8

Legend of the Dragon

Mortal Combat Armageddon

Scarface: The World is Yours

NOTE: Legend of the Dragon and Zelda is rated T for Teen. The Godfather, Scarface, and Mortal Combat is rated M for Mature. Both The Godfather and Scarface emulate scenes from their movies and the violence follows with them.. Mortal Combat was designed to appeal to an audience that's, "eager for violence."

Your Own Virtual World
Play God – Be God (Even If It's Only Electronically)

Part of the appeal of video games is the visual eye-candy that splashes across the television screen. But even the addictive imagery is only half of the equation. The remaining half is the magic bestowed upon our eyes when this imagery comes to life. Animation that's controlled by a gamer is all it takes to escape into a different time and place – a time and place brought to you by virtual reality.

As you can imagine, virtual reality is a hypothetical three-dimensional visual world created by a computer. Players can enter and move about in this world and interact with objects as if inside it. Some of the games that are already on the market give a pretty good idea of what virtual reality is and can do. Video games like Zelda, Halo, or Harry Potter allow players to enter into an environment and interact with objects, but they don't allow the player to create an environment and that's what virtual worlds are all about.

Without a single ounce of programming experience, anyone can create a virtual world and have loads of fun doing so. All one needs is an idea.

To begin, you'll want to construct a plan that maps your idea of the perfect world, the craziest world, or the oddest world that you can imagine. Some virtual world software will give you a template of sorts (a "starter" world) that lets you make additions and ultimately build a world that you've always dreamed of. A good example of template use is inside Maxis' SimCity or SimTown games. Both games provide pre-designed environments that provide plenty of space and opportunity to shape them into one that you prefer.

Of course, you could always start from scratch. The only problem with starting with scratch is that it takes more time and knowledge to add some of the features that virtual worlds provide. Either way (from scratch or from a template), most users build a world by adding objects and scenarios – even deleting some until they've reached the perfect balance.

A good place to find examples of what you could build in virtual world gaming is online. Every virtual world program available offers sample environments that players can download and install into their own system. Some manufacturers of these games even hold contests and award winners with free upgrades. Other suitable places to find ideas are from fiction books: -historical, -fantasy, -futuristic, you name it. Science fiction movies are a good resource for ideas as well.

Just understand that virtual gaming takes time. Rome wasn't built in a day and neither will your virtual world. There's no rush and this is a relaxing hobby. Take your time and have fun. Don't fret over not knowing how to build an object or lay down a map – you can learn how to do these kinds of things in due time. Your goal is to create a world of enjoyment and it won't help if you find yourself frustrated all the time.

When ready, you can add characters with their own unique histories, habits, strengths and weaknesses. You can even give them goals or small tasks to perform throughout the game. Giving your characters goals and tasks will help you give the game a plot.

To get started, look for RAD (Rapid Application Development) Tools. RAD tools will help you bang a virtual reality game together in no time and with little difficulty.